Your Biome Has Found You

poems by

Gloria Muñoz

Finishing Line Press
Georgetown, Kentucky

Your Biome Has Found You

for my family

Copyright © 2017 by Gloria Muñoz
ISBN 978-1-63534-190-4 First Edition
All rights reserved under International and Pan-American Copyright Conventions.
No part of this book may be reproduced in any manner whatsoever without written permission from the publisher, except in the case of brief quotations embodied in critical articles and reviews.

ACKNOWLEDGMENTS

"Your Biome has Found You" ~~ *50 Best New Poets*
"Thread by Thread" and "Entrañablemente" ~~ *Acentos Review*
"Red Alert" ~~ Forage Poetry

Publisher: Leah Maines

Editor: Christen Kincaid

Cover Art: Rose Muñoz

Author Photo: Kelley Jackson, Lucy Pearl Photography

Cover Design: Elizabeth Maines McCleavy

Printed in the USA on acid-free paper.
Order online: www.finishinglinepress.com
      also available on amazon.com

Author inquiries and mail orders:
Finishing Line Press
P. O. Box 1626
Georgetown, Kentucky 40324
U. S. A.

Table of Contents

Hieroglyphic Hug 1
First Night in the Little White Room 2
Echo Glass 3
Thread By Thread 4
On Death Rites 5
Naked With Scissors/Mother Cut Blue for Eyes/Green
    Grass Around Us 6
Book Hymn 7
Mother Machine 8
Second Night in the Little White Room 10
Red Alert 11
Alterations 13
Endangered 14
Four Ways of Looking at a Fish 16
Innate Skill 18
Defense Mechanism 20
Deficiency 21
Selenography 24
Wedding Dress Shopping on Madison Avenue 26
At the Totumo Mud Volcano 27
Light Pollution 28
The Veteran 30
The Taste of Salt 32
Entrañablemente 33
Your Biome Has Found You 34

HIEROGLYPHIC HUG

Within the first hours
of living a baby
is kangarooed into each
parent's skin to be reminded
of the womb and reconnected
to touch in an oxygenated world.

Perhaps, because the two
are so closely related, love
and hate come from the same place.
Love and hate: the worn
coat, the gloved hand
the tandem bicycle.
The symbol for an embrace
found in ancient Egyptian caves
resembles a nestling of lines,
one more crooked than the other,
one more shapeless.

The circumlocution of a hug
can be negotiated through distance
and the internet. On the train,
the street, the elevator, faces
avoid other faces. Crooked
and shapeless we nestle
our cellphones into us
like newborn kangaroos.

In hopes of solving our disconnectedness
the government will distribute coats
that fill with air to emulate a hug
to every lonely person in the country.

FIRST NIGHT IN THE LITTLE WHITE ROOM

Lick the cancer off my bones.
Suck out the marrow and chew on it.
Taste the rotting newborn cells,
settle and swell between your teeth.
Rub your longest finger across your gums. Taste it,
let it drip. Let it sting, tingle. Let it scorch
off the tip of your tongue. Think of poppies,
think of heroin. Glide your lips across
my purple eyelids. Slowly. Wake me up.

ECHO GLASS

I.
Walking on the damp lawn with a hand-cupped mirror tilted up—
her eyes, steady, watch the blue and white exhalations of the sky.
She steps through refracted clouds.

II.
Senos, the Spanish word for breasts
sounds like *Sueños*, which means dreams,
both are the subject of every tango ever written.

III.

Late some summer night
the rhinestoned sky glints galaxies
off their honeyed-skin,
peeling off one another, humid—
lying in the hush—he wants more time,
she wants her star map.

IV.
Light from stars takes so much time to reach our eyes.
We see them as they appeared hundreds, thousands
or even millions of years ago.

In an elevator's endless double-mirror she wonders
if she is gazing forward or back.

V.

She is more like the women in her family
than she would like to be.
When did she begin to say *yes* instead of *no*?
And why does she say *no* when she means *yes, please—yes*?

THREAD BY THREAD

> *I heard the incessant dissolving of silk—*
> *I felt my heart growing so old in real time.*
> —Agha Shahid Ali

You were born on a cloud-clogged night
to the ring of your own tintinnabular cry.
You were fed thread by thread by your mother.

You learned to love in another country
and the wind with its thousand hands
took what it could, and through star-clogged eyes

you watched dawn shake loose its skin—
and the saffron sun rained marigolds
as you gave yourself thread by thread to another.

Oh, body that is swept of its senses—you
learned to love with your brain and breath.
Your children will be born into the fog-clogged

years when you'll mend your mother like a doll
and bury your father, whose mind has unspooled
thread by thread to a child's. Cupping each word

like a stone, you'll wear your language like a family
heirloom. And your marigold chest will burn
when your grandchildren are born on a dream-clogged night
—you'll begin to dissolve thread by thread into the cross-stitched sky.

ON DEATH RITES

My father shows me the lake
he wants to be scattered in.
Remember, he says each time
we pass his lake.

My mother had me
help choose her mother's tombstone:
a gray marble slab—
carved rosary, *Elena*,
a plump angel's silhouette.

New burial trends
include being planted
as a tree or laced
into gun ammunition.

My ashes could feed the roots
of a sapling and shade my future
child, or aim steady at a head—
tear into the warm chest
of a deer falling to a bed
of pine needles.

NAKED WITH SCISSORS/MOTHER CUT BLUE FOR EYES/ GREEN GRASS AROUND US

Red iron rubs thigh
every part of my body
is screaming for you

Cherry blossoms dried
moonshine keeps us warm enough
chilled fingers climb up

The knife thrower's wife
cut her lover's hair last night
pricked her fingertip

Spiders suggest rain
you standing on my doorstep
I lock windows shut

Sun in inkblot eyes
driving down the beach I cried
a seagull hit glass

Rosary beads grow
in water he chokes on prayers
holy exorcism

Magenta wild lips
tangled pant leg drove her mad
she laid on the tracks

BOOK HYMN
> *Have you the little chest—to put the alive—in?*
> —Emily Dickinson

A profile is made
by what is retracted:
the slope, groove,
the crest. How air holds
skin, which holds hollows
stretched thinly
to contain each character
together. The hero's
chin is a fickle one.
The antagonist's
brow is insecure.

In this scene
I am the faceless
ingénue. Here, I
will be the first to say
I have forgotten you.
I'm in a constant *déjà vu*
as the plot thickens
by folding further into itself.

Tell me Don Quixote
was right all along.
& the windmills were giants
& the farm girls,
fair maidens &
the donkey, a stead
& the lunatic,
a knight, or, the knight,
a lunatic. & if I fold into
myself, fold into myself,
fold into—would you carry me?
In the grass I'm listening to bees
stinging other bees.

MOTHER MACHINE
sestina

Foot-pedal tilting below the skirt. Their eyes
on the needle the metal the thread the cloth.
Sliding through jabs a fish spine cuts
through inches of air—then little one rises
and whirls above unwinding spool,
barefoot she dances round mother machine.

A bundle of bees tinkers inside the machine's
engine—they are silver & bolt-eyed
& buzzing through the shedding spool,
wedding cloth to cloth
with a prick & rise—& a prick & rise—
their stingers strike tiny fires that cut

into her purple lungs.   With each new cut
the mother makes—the daughter is more machine,
less girl, breathless   pulseless   she rises.
Or, is she fuller of breath when her eyes
of mirror & candlewick witness the cloth's
communion to thread?   & the spool

how its silk leaks, how its song pools
into the room, where the mother cuts
through her nocturnal tears by running the cloth
of paisley & peacock through the mechanic
jaw while her somnambular wide-eyed
daughter (who hums like a bee) rises

above the house   she rises
higher, higher, unspooling
into the noctilucent clouds. Starlit, she eyes
the tiny house & listens for the gliding cut's
exhale, exhale.   She fears the mechanism
that anchors her kite of cloth

& bone to her mother, who cut her of a cloth
too similar to her's. How can the daughter rise, how can the daughter rise
through the droning bleat of the machine
that drains the bleeding spool
drop by drop without ever cutting
it away, so it can get away from the eyes

that mechanic & idle unspool into piles of cloth
while the girl rises cutting   away from the mother
(who every night threads her sadness through the needle's eye)?

SECOND NIGHT IN THE LITTLE WHITE ROOM

In the corner, there is a cloth bag hanging
from the ceiling with two holes for eyes. In it,
         a head, of a man, of a cow, of a horse, my horse,
         the white one, with the Spanish gait.
I can see him winning a race. Pink spotted nostrils
weep blood on the floor. He has come back so old,
         and I, like a child, an infant, a sad fetus, force fed
         by this cord. My body floats on the surface
of his black bubble eyes, I want to touch, squeeze,
swallow them whole. Let them rattle in me.
         Let them pop. I want to thank him, the bastard,
         for coming to see me wet my bed.

RED ALERT

Beijing. 4 a.m. We are greeted by smog
and nosebleeds. Prepared to fly
another 13 hours suspended
in the jaundiced sky, strapped
in a steel bird of compressed air.
Breath in—unzip, expand, sit back
and watch the grandmas with wet towels
draped over their heads,
the babies in puffer coats, squawking.

It is warm everywhere else this winter,
yet, we are in a tundra of recycled air.
They sell canned fresh-mountain air
for countries like this. I know
because the man sitting next to us in the terminal says
he was on the verge of inventing it in the 80's.
Oh, his middle-aged remorse!
But hey, we're all on the cusp

of inventing something. Aren't we?
The canned air is made real
by the number of facemasks in the airport.
I recall all the smudged data
from the world's largest carbon polluter
and laugh while crying into my bottle
of French Alps' seltzer (not in the chantepleure manner
but in the wake-me-up-from-this-nightmare kind of way).

10 a.m. Back on a plane
and back to my nosebleed, crusty and pulsing.
When we are high enough, I watch T.V.
There's an infomercial of a Japanese woman—
iridescent and tired—selling beauty products.
She rubs on a mask and then (as time passes instantly on T.V.)
she peels off the film and looks firmer,

brighter. She repeats the process, peels
another sticky layer away, she now has wider eyes
and makeup on and highlights, her skin is lighter.
Again, she peels and a different woman appears altogether:
a blonde American celebrity, all lashes and lip-gloss
floods the screen. She peels once more
and our two-story plane is jostled
as the seatbelt announcement cuts the static
in four languages.

I'm sitting next to my dear friend Eva, a doula
who believes there are too many people on earth,
she is on antidepressants.
"If such and such becomes president,
I am definitely moving," she says.
Sigh. Eye roll. She is always on the brink of moving.
But, we are all on the brink of something. Aren't we?

ALTERATIONS

1.
I imagine the skin on the ridge of your nose would be the easiest to slice
but the incision must be made on the inner rim of the nostrils
to hide any sign of alteration. Then, the skin is scythed from fibrous gristle
and peeled off like a damp glove.

If your nose is too hunched, its crest can be sanded
to a delicate slope. If your nose is too flat, a mountain range
can be grafted and cinched at the tip.

2.
I'll draw the line first in the fold of the lid, to extract
the blinking flesh—lift and pull and sew and while
we're here, we might as well slit the edge-seams further.

Your wider eyes will be waiting lifted and bruised
—soon shiny translucent rinds will expose
enviable lychees ripening in the sockets.

3.
If your face is too full, open your mouth fish-wide limp
and I'll carve your contour—as my scalpel curves around
your dreaming of ancestors. Let your phlegm swing pendulum
in your throat as my tweezers pull the excess fat and lineage
from your cheeks and chin.

4.
I'll snip the muscle below your toddler's tongue
to help silken his consonants and vowels.
To allow him to lick fully the syntax, to savor
the language of success, to flex and flare
his tongue to say *what   who   where* and *ready*.

ENDANGERED

There are too many padlocks
in this gridlocked neighborhood,
you can't even trust your neighbors
anymore—let alone walk home after school.

Mothers pull their children closer
when they see you pass,
as if you were made of tar—
a sticky leprosy that will never leave

them or this precious neighborhood.
I grew up here too, you want to say
—but you look down.
You are expected to be controversial

so you keep your eyes focused
on the weeds growing
between the sidewalk
slabs. Those persistent tufts of green

wedging their way into existence.
You are just walking vigilant, alone,
eyes locked two feet ahead on the ground,
quicker now. Not too fast,

must not make anyone uncomfortable.
You think, *these weeds, I get them,*
for even in broad daylight,
they too are threatening and invisible.

Your pulse and steps sharpen, almost home.
You think of Trayvon, why can't you stop
thinking of him? Why can't you stop thinking?
He was 17, just like you, walking alone—exposed.

Why did he have his black ass out at night anyway?
You think and try to focus on your rapid steps.
*And, what on earth was that watchful watchman
watching for?*

A black man? A teenager?
Was someone watching you right now?
You want so badly to stop thinking
about this teen you didn't even know,

about his parents, about your brother (who is darker-
skinned than you and so naïve), of the night
your father's vehicle was searched with you strapped
into a car-seat shaking, of the countless times

you've watched people flinch
or cross the street when they see you.
I can't breathe—you realize
as you pass out on the bright Florida sidewalk.

Will someone come help this black boy
get some water? Will anyone help this black boy?

FOUR WAYS OF LOOKING AT FISH

1.
Line them up on their sides.
Keep your knees soft, tilting
for balance, hovering over

their creamy iridescent bodies,
that glint against the teak floorboards.

Begin Striking
their unnumbered heads
with a tool, called a priest.

They will be silent with one
unblinking eye.

Watch them, watch you watch them draining
into the teak floorboards.

2.
The salmon run is a sequined frenzy pulsing against time,
through thousands of upstream miles
of infinite heartbeats. Fueling
themselves with their chainmail
skin they transform into scarlet
arrows magnetized toward the familiar
smell of home to spawn, to die
to begin again on their natal gravel grounds.

3.
Have you heard the one about the fish and the coins,
the fish with a belly-full of magic; the fish with a gold ring
fish, bountiful
fish, magnificent
fish, who loves with an open mouth
fish, thrown back into water, dead
fish, thrown back, alive
hind-legged fish who walked to shore
prophetic fish
spiny fish, poisonous delicacy
fish, mysterious with a light
dangling from its head
like a small moon lurking
in the deep sea-space?

4.
Our earliest ancestors swam
and we all hang umbilical.
We grow legs,
separate our fingers
and are suddenly
reeled into living.

INNATE SKILL

With feet and knees flared and palms facing
the ceiling, I'm lying on my back, with my lips

slightly parted, with my eyes mostly closed.
My yoga teacher gleams

when she tells me I've gotten better at savasana,
at being a corpse. I won the best sleeper award

in kindergarten— a running family joke,
my first academic achievement.

My nephews are read to and sung to
as they fall asleep each night,

so they will be kept, so they will wake up.
Lullabies are meant to prepare people for dying.

In corpse pose on the wooden floor, every inhale
buries me, the ebb and flow of it all engulfs me

the small of my back is the only thing that retains
its curve— a twilight sky, a rabbit's hole, a tombstone.

In Spanish twice, in English once, as a child I prayed
to Mary, to Jesus, to God. My metronomic bedtime

ritual. Children grow calm hearing their parents sing,
sleep, sleep, there's nothing to fear—

each withheld vowel, a tiny cry—pleading.
Lying face up in a room full of people

imitating corpses. The class breathes
a collective reprieve as we learn to live

with death scratching at the backs of our hands.

DEFENSE MECHANISM
> *All things that are, are equally removed from being nothing.*
> —John Donne

I am a pessimist who tries
to see the bright side of things
through a sooted windowpane,
to focus on the water filling half
the glass without being concerned
with the billions of dust particles
or the crack at the bottom of the glass.
Still, everything reminds me

of global warming and of our inevitable
self-destruction. I think things through,
read instructions—learning that sleeping
the right amount of time (eight hours
for someone my age) will extend my life,
finding that eating this and not that will help
my chances of not getting cancer.

At a red light I am smashed
into the side of my car as I skid
across four lanes. I cross
the street and become a flower
pressed into the ground by a raging bus.
My thanatophobic anxiety leads me
to an over-thinking-sweaty-place at 3 a.m.
Unlike the opossum, I cannot play dead,

nor can my body coil into an armored
shell. I lack the venom-tipped spines, the beak, the fangs,
the rib cage that breaks and breaks to spear
to protect, the bioluminescent jelly flesh, the cryptic
coloration. The long skin that holds
all my bones—while I'm walking,
driving, dreaming—seems rather thin. Yet,
coming up for breath after getting pummeled
by the sea again reminds me that I am not
ready to become a small nameless thing,
another kind of small plural thing.

DEFICIENCY

When I return from living
in India, I am informed
of my deficiency, that my body
could develop an autoimmune
disorder, that I could experience
a series of symptoms including:
fatigue, depression, anxiety,
weight gain, low body
temperatures, and infertility.

Twice a week I chant
Om as I stare at a lamp
grafted from a salt mine
located in India, Nepal
or Pakistan. The yoga studio
also sells an organic, non-GMO,
pink Himalayan salt cup.
Its eighty-four minerals,
one of which is iodine,
promise to heal and internally
cleanse. *Om*—

I chant and think of Kali,
who, while I was in India,
became my Hindu patron saint.
Kali, with her red long tongue
and her black eyes and her garland
of fifty severed heads. Kali,
who represents freedom
and destruction, whose fearless wrath
devoured time, whose girdle
of severed arms frees
her devotees of their karma,
who dances wild on the battlefield
to redeem the universe and its cosmos.

And I, who drank the tap water,
who was off my malaria pills
for the last four months,
who walked barefoot
on temple and cave
floors that were sticky
with jasmine petals and goat blood,
who, on more than one occasion,
smoked hashish on rooftops,
I developed an iodine deficiency?

We import pink rocks
from Himalayan foothills
to make soap, deodorant,
bath salts, rock lamps, candle
holders, bookends and gourmet table salt.
Half of all children born every year
in India have severe iodine deficiencies,
and, in turn, brain damage,
deaf mutism, dwarfism
and developmental depletion.

I imagine Kali with her matted dreads
emerging from a salt mine,
clawing at her blue breasts,
Kali the destructor. Her tremendous tears
monsoon over the mountains
of salt like a thousand-headed cobra
striking proudly and instinctively—
leaving behind a pink salt landslide,
a burial for the miners and their families,
depleting us all of iodine.
But who am I to blame Kali,
or to reduce a goddess to a patron saint?

Om I chant with 28 women and men
clad in spandex twisting and sweating

and breathing, reaching for something
like fulfillment. If Kali came into the room
she'd stamp out our incense and tear
out our throat chakras to cease
our incessant *Oms*. Kali, with her bloody
scythe and golden trident. Kali,
whose body is bathed in ash,
whose wide third eye pierces through
the past and present and future
of us all to reduce us back
to what we really are—
water, salt, water, salt.

SELENOGRAPHY

Again this morning drops repeatedly tap the metal
box outside my window and I wake to these sounds of water and Q train
track announcer telling me it's 9:15 on Friday, October 9th
and that the next stop is 7th Avenue, riding the train,
now a quarter to eleven, on the wet bridge over the river
out of a window I admire another brick bridge and make a list of to-do's
starting with calling mother, who's enrolled in a writing class
and has left me six messages, each asking for help—though I'll call
only after five, until then I sell books to strangers
past the twin lions, through library doors, downstairs
along freshly mopped marble floors arranging the hard-covers
and tending to customers, each of whom buys both books,
($90)— I nod, smile and wonder what they'll learn
from a dialogue between a neuroscientist and a modern dancer;
the topic of their conversation is phenomenology—
as this is revealed I bite my lip and watch the audience
hmm and *ooh*, some cock their heads to one side, others hold chins
between thumb and forefinger—and after selling out
I walk through an evening drizzle to the East Village
to meet Alice for coffee; I order hot cocoa instead,
and welcome the warmth as we talk about our weeks and plans
for better jobs which resolves nothing, then we head uptown
to see her boyfriend in a play about the Israeli Palestinian Conflict,
in which he was cast as an Anti-Semitic cartoon mouse,
and I count the blue lights hanging from the black-box ceiling,
leave at intermission and ride the train back over the bridge,
on my street I'm greeted by kids jumping into the spray
of a broken hydrant, as I walk upstairs, my phone rings,
it's my mother and she is crying
she asks if I've read the paper *did you see what they did to the moon?*
men are always looking for water or oil somewhere—I know it's important
for science but I just can't believe it—my mother,
who, among other Hindu and Christian gods,

has always talked and prayed to the moon,
I've watched meditate under eclipses and cut her hair—
right now I can't tell if she's mad at the scientists or at me,
standing in front of my window I search for her face in clouded sky.

WEDDING DRESS SHOPPING ON MADISON AVENUE

I gave in to Val, who loves bridal
T.V. shows, whose eyes luster
with silent-movie-ingénue-sparkle
whenever we talk about weddings.

The inside of the brownstone glows
with faux candlelight, the attendants,
all French, wear tight black buns,
dress suits and rosy acrylic nails.

Within minutes Val has her arm piled
with sample dresses ranging from size 0 to14,
she is smiling with her teeth. I am rushed to
be fit into an overly padded strapless bra

that spans the length of my torso.
The attendant holds my hand as I step
into the billowing beaded tulle. When I open the door
and step onto a platform, Val gasps

and begins to inhale deeply
to keep from crying.
In the back of the store dangling
from a wall of mounted hooks,
veils hang like hunted rabbits.

AT THE TOTUMO MUD VOLCANO

Plunging into the insatiable mouth of the earth
to be suspended in the O of anticipation—before the deluge,
before the rupture. Disintegrating, buoyant—cupped in a throat
full of cement—feet cannot reach the pit of her stomach,
which has plummeted abysmally through the frothing and fermenting
mineral stew, hands cannot climb her scattered spine,
lips cannot help but let seep in
as a stranger, with her grandmother's olivine eyes, pushes her
beneath the mud—and there, deaf to the mad gibber of tourists,
to the boil and sizzle of molten matter,
to the shifting of tectonic plates, to the myth and past of this place.
She fears the kettledrum that beats tribal and resonates off her inner rib.
Spilling out one cell at a time, she is coreless, boundless, shadowless.
Yet, when she surfaces, a phosphorescent flock of sheep buds
from her mouth and her aqueous eyes pour open
to reflect the double image of a boy holding a camera.

LIGHT POLLUTION

Fireflies are endangered
—they don't know why,
could be pesticides or light
pollution preventing
them from finding their mates.

This is what keeps me
up again tonight,
on the eve of my birthday.
I read brain cells stop
regenerating now.

The fan drags its whirr
across the ceiling, dust
filters gilded from the streetlight.
Most of our grandparents
are dead. Or, nearly there.

They are quieter now
and less wise.
My grandmother sews
and chews in slow motion.
Her right frontal lobe

is a meshwork of swollen white
matter. She's an effigy who stares
at each grandchild before saying
a name. She, like most of us,
is some combination of happy and sad.

There is a body resting
next to me, one I love.
Love, the construct that drove Dante
through hell to reach his moon.
When did I become someone's

keeper? Minding, mending. We live
on a nature preserve,
manicured and monitored.
I can see a neon 24-hour car wash
from the living room window.

It reminds me of the subway track
we once lived next to,
always lit, humming.
There are whale songs
in my ears tonight.
The bluish yowls resonate

through my fingertips.
My cell phone strobes and seizers
on my nightstand. I want to thank
friends and family for calling in these
first hours of my new year

but, I am occupied counting
how many whale skeletons must lay
cradled at the bottom of the ocean.
And mapping constellations
through the ceiling,

I know there is less phantasmagoria,
less starlight, only lost hearts
flickering in the dark.

THE VETERAN PARKED IN HIS WHEELCHAIR AT THE INTERSECTION WITH HIS GOLDEN RETRIEVER AT HIS FEET ABUSES THE PAPER-BAGGED BOTTLE WHILE HOLDING A SIGN THAT SAYS: "I'LL TAKE ANYTHING"—

he looks like a blue-eyed
version of my grandfather,
who resented the homeless
because they were not a part
of the America he envisioned
in the 70's. They were left out
of his letters and phone calls
home—for they, with their grit
and cardboard and frenetic:
*please, a dollar, a meal,
for my children, et cetera*
reminded him of the cave of memories
he lived in. My grandfather,

who, in disenchanted-fairy-tale-speed,
went from being a South American politician
to a mechanic in Queens.
A month before dying he tried to live
out the American dream, buying
his children computers, vacuums,
televisions, becoming a better
Christian, a better husband,
undoing his fathering
with gifts and rosaries,
so he would not be
misremembered.

For half a year my mother kept
his glasses in her purse,
along with her library card,
which she used twice a week.
She frequented the first floor
where she once sat with her ailing father

looking up random newspaper
articles on the microfiche.

A squint-eyed homeless man
now wears my grandfather's
tortoiseshell glasses. She brings him coffee
twice a week and, near the periodicals,
they exchange news about
the weather, their families,
their losses, et cetera.

THE TASTE OF SALT

There are craters on the beach,
war fossils. The sea is still
and humming green.
Our faces are gilded peach
as we watch the amber sun
plunge beyond the line
that makes the world seem flat,

leaving behind a purple sky
spangled with extinguishing armies
of fireflies. Seagulls cry
their whooping song
as we run deeper into the mouth
of the whale. We arrive at the temple ruins,

the garden of crustaceans
and armless wonders. There hangs a crippled
hand, there, a couple entwined
like fighting snakes. Beneath the belly
of the stone jaguar we whitewash
an enormous lobster.

Each brushstroke peels its color
until it's a handful of sand.
We are left red with the taste of salt
on our tongues. A family of peacocks pecks
at the body of a woman whose head
is replaced by a gold-leafed star.

Sitting under a Jackfruit tree we find
the elephant-headed boy-god.
With tailbones in the air, our foreheads
touch the ground and we worship
with bent knees, hitting temples with knuckles,
pulling earlobes and begging for wisdom—
in the distance bombs shake loose of their shells.

ENTRAÑABLEMENTE

To love another
with your entire being,
so much so that you feel
it in your entrails.

The English definition
leaves the taste of entrails
in the air. In Spanish,
it's a murmur between sheets
of ocean; the crepuscular peeling
of dusks and dawns; it is lungs
falling down three flights of stairs;
eyes drunk with the Milky
Way's dust and honey;
the electric currents of two
bodies that produce their own
magnetic field, their own rotation
among the humming string
of planets; the equinoctial
throbbing of the tide;
the gargantuan wrestling
of the squid and the whale—
who, tangled and dying,
need one another.

YOUR BIOME HAS FOUND YOU

And who will kiss open
the spine of the resurrection fern
that's hunched like a widow, hunched
like a shamed child? How it locks and hides
and browns under the sun—a laborer's
hands picking blistered tomatoes,
or a pile of bones, perhaps bird bones
—small, dry, silent.

        Here is the damp and thickest marsh
        of your interior wetland. And here,
        begins your tundra of moss, rock and shrub.
        Here is the thing you lost,
        perhaps the saddest or loveliest thing
        —remember? It was suddenly taken—as a fish
        spine is plucked from its open body on an open plate.
        And who will pry apart the arms

of the praying mantis who preys on her
lover? Who will resuscitate the tiny
bird whose head rests on a fallen nest? You
are helpless and wild here. A murmuration
of starlings pulses in your chest. A soundtrack
of breeding amphibians seeps through you. Cicadas
scream petrified from treetops. The feral sounds
of wilderness sharpen your teeth.

        It is November, goldfish scales crunch
        under your soles, the autumnal scent
        of a fire inhales you,
        the aerials are coming and going.
        While adding up all the dead things you carry,
        you realize, there is so much dirt in you.
        Still, your nautilus ears listen, waiting
        to hear your native sea.

Gloria Muñoz is a writer, translator and educator whose writing has appeared in publications including *The Best New Poets Anthology, Acentos Review, The Sarah Lawrence Review, The Brooklyn Review, Entropy, Forage, Salt Creek Journal, Poems2Go,* and the *Going Om* anthology. Her writing has been honored by the Estelle J. Zbar Poetry Prize, the Bettye Newman Poetry Award, the New York Summer Writer's Institute Fellowship and the Think Small to Think Big Artist Grant.

Gloria is a co-founder of Pitch Her Productions, a nonprofit dedicated to supporting women in the arts. She teaches creative writing at Eckerd College in Saint Petersburg, Florida.

www.ingramcontent.com/pod-product-compliance
Lightning Source LLC
LaVergne TN
LVHW041559070426
835507LV00011B/1181